What-to-Do Guides for Kids®

What to Do When You WORRY TOO MUCH

A Kid's Guide to Overcoming Anxiety

by Dawn Huebner, Ph.D.

illustrated by Bonnie Matthews

MAGINATION PRESS • WASHINGTON, D.C.

Published by
MAGINATION PRESS®
An Educational Publishing Foundation Book
American Psychological Association
750 First Street, NE
Washington, DC 20002

Magination Press is a registered trademark of the American Psychological Association.
For more information about our books, including a complete catalog, please write to us,
call 1-800-374-2721, or visit our website at www.apa.org/pubs/magination.

Library of Congress Cataloging-in-Publication Data

Huebner, Dawn.
What to do when you worry too much : a kid's guide to overcoming anxiety / by Dawn Huebner ;
illustrated by Bonnie Matthews.
p. cm. — ("What to do" guides for kids)
Summary: "Teaches school-age children cognitive-behavioral techniques to reduce and overcome
anxiety, fears, and worry, with writing and drawing activities and self-help exercises and strategies.
Includes introduction for parents"—Provided by publisher.
ISBN 1-59147-314-4 (pbk. : alk. paper)
1. Worry in children—Juvenile literature. 2. Anxiety in children—Juvenile literature.
I. Matthews, Bonnie. II. Title. III. Series.
BF723.W67H84 2006
155.4'1246—dc22
2005017523

Manufactured in the United States of America
23

CONTENTS

Introduction to Parents and Caregivers

If you are the parent or caregiver of an anxious child, you know what it feels like to be held hostage. So does your child. Children who worry too much are held captive by their fears. They go to great lengths to avoid frightening situations, and ask the same anxiety-based questions over and over again. Yet the answers give them virtually no relief. Parents and caregivers find themselves spending huge amounts of time reassuring, coaxing, accommodating, and doing whatever else they can think of to minimize their child's distress.

But it doesn't work. The anxiety remains in control. As you have undoubtedly discovered, simply telling an anxious child to stop worrying doesn't help at all. Nor does applying adult logic, or allowing your child to avoid feared situations, or offering reassurance every time the fears are expressed.

Anxiety has a way of growing, spreading, shifting in form, and generally resisting efforts to talk it out of existence. But there is hope. *What to Do When You Worry Too Much* will teach you and your child a new and more successful way to think about and manage anxiety. The techniques described in this book will help your child take control.

You and your child are accustomed to dealing with anxiety in a particular way.

Changing these patterns will take some time and will require diligence on both of your parts. Reminding your child to use the techniques presented here is one of the most important things you can do. Use humor when you can. Stay positive, and encourage all efforts in the right direction.

A basic understanding of the psychology underlying the techniques presented in this book will help you to most effectively coach your child. All of the techniques are based on cognitive-behavioral principles used extensively by therapists to reduce widespread anxiety. The techniques have been adapted to children and are presented with explanations that will make sense to them, but you might find yourself wondering how or why these things work.

The techniques in this book are based on three principles known as *containment*, *externalization*, and *competing demands*. To understand containment, begin by picturing a gallon of milk. In its carton, a gallon of milk doesn't take up much space. You can put it on the counter or into the refrigerator and go about your business. Now imagine that same gallon of milk without the carton. Uncontained, it would make a huge puddle that you would endlessly be stepping around or through. What a mess!

Anxiety is like that gallon of milk. Without a container, it spreads out and becomes nearly impossible to avoid. Anxiety needs to be contained. Creating a Worry Box and scheduling Worry Time, described in the chapter "Spending Less Time on Worries," are the psychological equivalents of keeping milk in a jug rather than letting it run all over the floor.

Next, think of anxiety with a capital A, as if it were a separate entity with its own name rather than an integral part of your child. Think of Anxiety or The Worry as an unwanted visitor that you and your child are tired of hosting. This book will teach your child to see it this way, too. Externalizing anxiety in this way sets the stage for exerting control over it, as described in the chapter "Talking Back To Worries."

The principle of competing demands holds that a person can't be both relaxed and anxious at the same time. Staying involved in something fun is a powerful deterrent to anxiety. Distraction is one of the most useful tools a child can use to break

free from anxiety. When a child is absorbed in playing with toys, testing his wits against a computer game, riding her bike, and so forth, there is less room for The Worry to creep back in, even if nothing about the feared situation has changed.

What to Do When You Worry Too Much will be most effective when read out loud. Sit with your child, read slowly, look at the pictures, and do the activities as directed. Read just one or two chapters at a time. Wait a day or two before moving on in the book, as children need time to absorb new ideas and practice new strategies.

There is often a genetic component to anxiety, which means that if you are the parent of an anxious child, you might be an anxious person, too. Feel free to join with your child in using the worry-fighting techniques described in this book. The basic principles work as well with adults as they do with children.

If, however, you feel highly anxious in response to your child's anxiety, you might find it helpful to consult with a therapist, who will be able to provide you and your child with some additional guidance and support. Please also consult with a therapist if anxiety is significantly interfering with your child's life.

From the moment you present this book to your child, remember the power of positive thinking. Maintain faith in your child's ability to grow strong against The Worry. Project an air of confidence. You are moving toward the day when you will be able to say that your child *used* to worry too much, but not any more. Won't that feel good?

CHAPTER ONE

Are You Growing Worries?

Most things grow when you tend to them.

Have you ever planted a tomato seed?
If you cover your seed with rich,
dark soil and water it and make sure
it gets plenty of sunlight, pretty soon
a little green shoot will appear.

If you give it
more water each day,
the green shoot will turn
into a big stalk with
leaves and flowers.
And then one day,
a tomato will appear!

If you keep tending
to your plant, more
and more tomatoes will
appear. Soon you will
have so many tomatoes that you
might have to go to the library for a tomato cookbook
so you can learn to make tomato sauce and tomato soup.

Tomatoes will appear in your salad and next to your tuna fish. You will find tomato sandwiches in your lunchbox, tomato juice for a snack, and tomato pasta for dinner. And one day, there will be so many tomatoes that your dad will suggest chopping them up to make tomato ice cream and tomato cookies!

All of those tomatoes will have come from one little seed that you planted and tended every day.

Draw something that you have helped to grow.

Did you know that worries are like tomatoes? No, you can't eat them. But you can make them grow, simply by paying attention to them.

Many children tend to their worries, even though they don't really mean to. And pretty soon, what might have started as just a little seed of worry has become a HUGE PILE OF PROBLEMS that you don't know how to get rid of.

If this has happened to you,
if your worries have grown so big that
they bother you almost every day,
then this book is for you.

The bad news, as you know,
is that worries can grow pretty fast
and cause a lot of trouble.

The good news, which you may
not know, is that you have the power
to make the worries go away. You do.

Keep reading and you will learn how.

CHAPTER TWO

What Is a Worry?

Grown-ups sometimes call worries anxiety or stress. People who worry a lot are said to be NERVOUS or ANXIOUS.

Whatever you call it, a worry is a thought that upsets you and makes you feel bad inside.

A worry can be a specific thought that makes you feel scared, like "What if Mom forgets to pick me up after my soccer practice?" Or it can be more general, like getting a FLUTTERY, sick feeling in your stomach every day before school, even though you aren't quite sure what is upsetting you.

Everyone feels worried sometimes.

It's normal to feel worried on your way to the doctor if you think you might be getting a SHOT, or before a SPELLING TEST if the words are really hard. Most kids worry a little if they are having a NEW SITTER watch them for the first time, or if they have to walk into a DARK ROOM with no lights on at all.

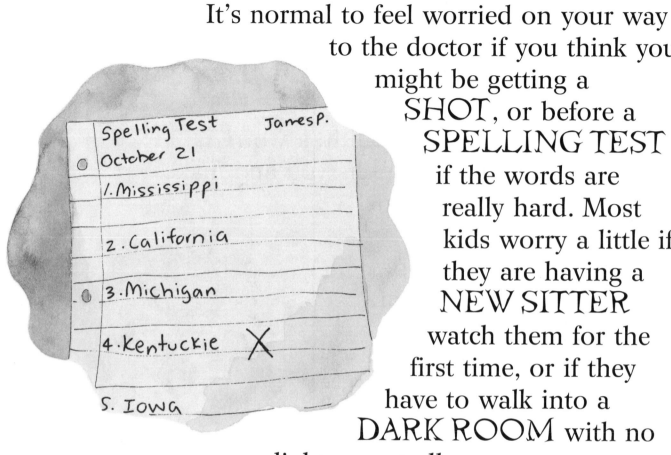

Lots of worries don't make sense, though, like worries about MONSTERS, which don't really exist. Or worries about NO ONE LIKING YOU, when you know that kids play with you every day.

Whether or not a worry makes sense to other people, it sure seems real to the person who is feeling it. And isn't it nice when a hug or some reassurance makes the worry go away?

But some worries don't go away.

Kids who have trouble with worries find that their worries get stuck. Even if their mom or dad is always there to get them after soccer practice, even if they aren't due for a shot at the doctor's office, or even if they have had fun with the sitter in the past, the worries just go on and on.

Draw something that you worry about.

If you are reading this book, you are probably a kid whose worries get stuck. You probably have worries that other people don't quite understand. And your worries probably last longer than other people think they should. People probably say, "Don't worry about it" all the time, but it isn't easy for you to just stop worrying.

It isn't easy.

But it is possible.

Once you learn a little more about worries, you'll be ready to start working on making your worries go away.

CHAPTER THREE

How Do Worries Get Started?

Seeing or hearing about something scary can make a worry get started. Watching POLICE SHOWS or MOVIES WITH BAD GUYS can make kids think that something bad is going to happen to them.

Sometimes bad things really do happen, like someone dies or parents get divorced or your best friend stops liking you.

When something scary or sad happens, or when you hear something that makes you think that something scary or sad could happen, worries can get started.

Difficult or disappointing things happen to everyone from time to time. Many kids feel bad for a while, and then they start thinking of something to cheer themselves up. Some kids are good at reassuring themselves and finding ways to solve their own problems. Often, kids can talk to someone, and then they feel better. But some kids—kids a lot like you—might try to do these very same things and they still end up worrying.

Sometimes kids who worry a lot have a mom or dad or some other relative who also worries a lot. The tendency to worry is something you can be born

 with, just like you are born with a certain eye color or the ability to curl your tongue.

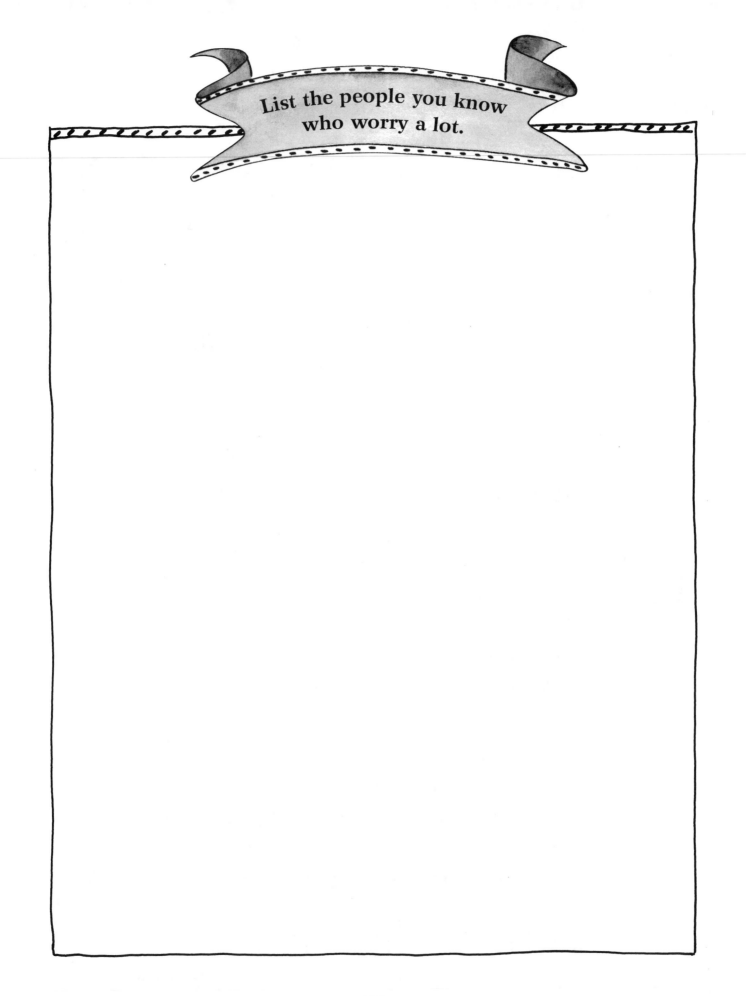

List the people you know
who worry a lot.

Some people think that worries are
ALL IN YOUR HEAD,
but they are not!

If you are a child who worries a
lot, you know that worries can make
your body feel bad. Worries can
cause a sick feeling inside. They can
make your stomach hurt, and make
your head ache, too. They can make
you sweaty and cause your heart to
pound. Worries can make you feel
shaky or dizzy, like you are going to
faint or throw up. Actually, some kids
have these bad feelings in their
bodies and don't even realize that
worries are causing them!

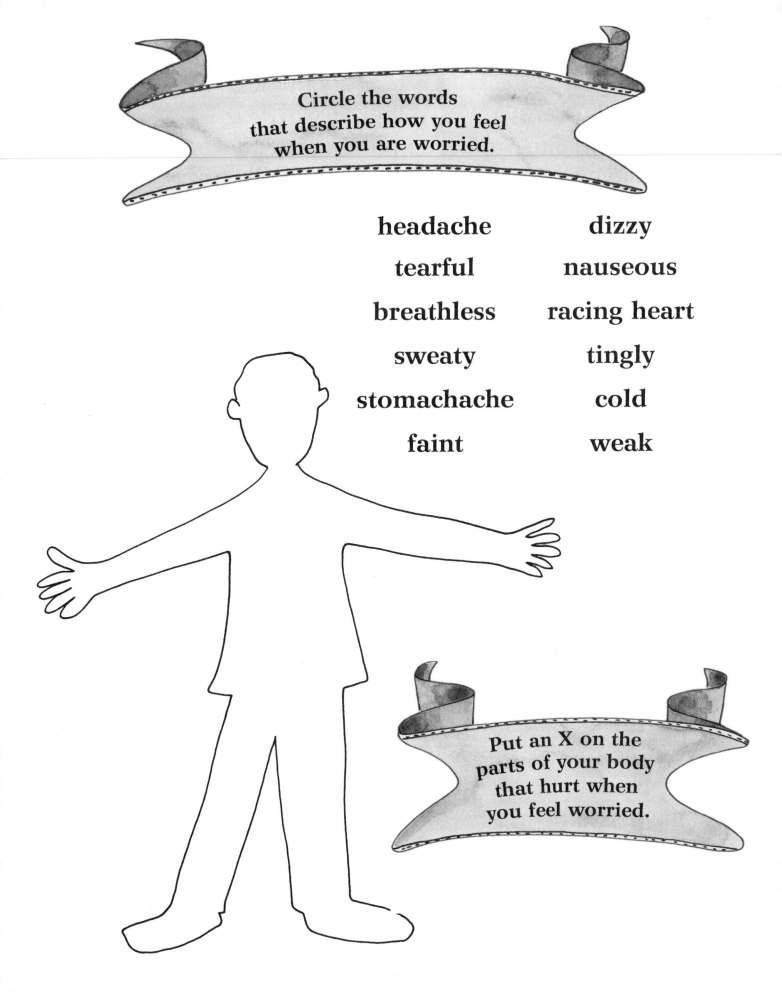

Circle the words
that describe how you feel
when you are worried.

headache	dizzy
tearful	nauseous
breathless	racing heart
sweaty	tingly
stomachache	cold
faint	weak

Put an X on the
parts of your body
that hurt when
you feel worried.

No one wants to have lots of worries. It isn't any fun, and it can make your body feel bad. Did you know that worries can cause other problems, too?

Kids who worry a lot often feel best when they are right next to their mom or dad or someone else they know really well. They avoid things that other kids think are fun, like going on SLEEPOVERS or PLAYING AT FRIENDS' HOUSES.

Kids who worry a lot have trouble doing things that other kids can do more easily. It is hard for them to get on the bus to go to school or to fall asleep alone. So kids who worry a lot miss out on things that other kids get to do.

Even worse, kids who worry a lot find that grown-ups get kind of mad at them.

Moms get ANNOYED when you ask the same worry questions over and over again.

Dads get TIRED and GROUCHY when your worries make it hard for you to sleep on your own.

Teachers get FRUSTRATED when you say you need to go to the nurse every day because your stomach always hurts.

25

Has someone gotten MAD at you for problems caused by your worries?

Draw that person looking mad.

Well, enough about the
bad news about worries.
Now let's talk about how to
make your worries go away.

Making Worries Go Away

The first thing to do when you have a worry is put it into words. You can talk to yourself about the worry. Or you can find a helpful person, like your mom or dad, to talk to about it.

Then use LOGIC to make the worry less powerful.

Logic is when you think about what is really true instead of what you're afraid might happen.

Logic is reminding yourself that really bad things don't happen very often.

Logic is knowing that even if something that's a little bit bad does happen, you can get through it.

When you use logic, you can make a plan that helps you feel calmer and less worried.

Pretend you're a kid who is afraid of DOGS because you think they might jump up and bite you. If you were invited to a new friend's house to play, you would probably start to worry right away. You would think, "What if she has a dog?" or "What if her dog bites me?" You might even decide not to go, because you definitely do not want to get bitten.

Before you spend any more time worrying, try to use logical thinking. First of all, your friend might not even have a dog! Asking about the details and getting answers can save a lot of time and worry.

If you find out that your friend does have a dog, you can make sure she knows ahead of time that dogs make you nervous. Maybe your friend can hold on to the dog while you get to know it and see that it is gentle. Or maybe the dog can be put outside while you are there.

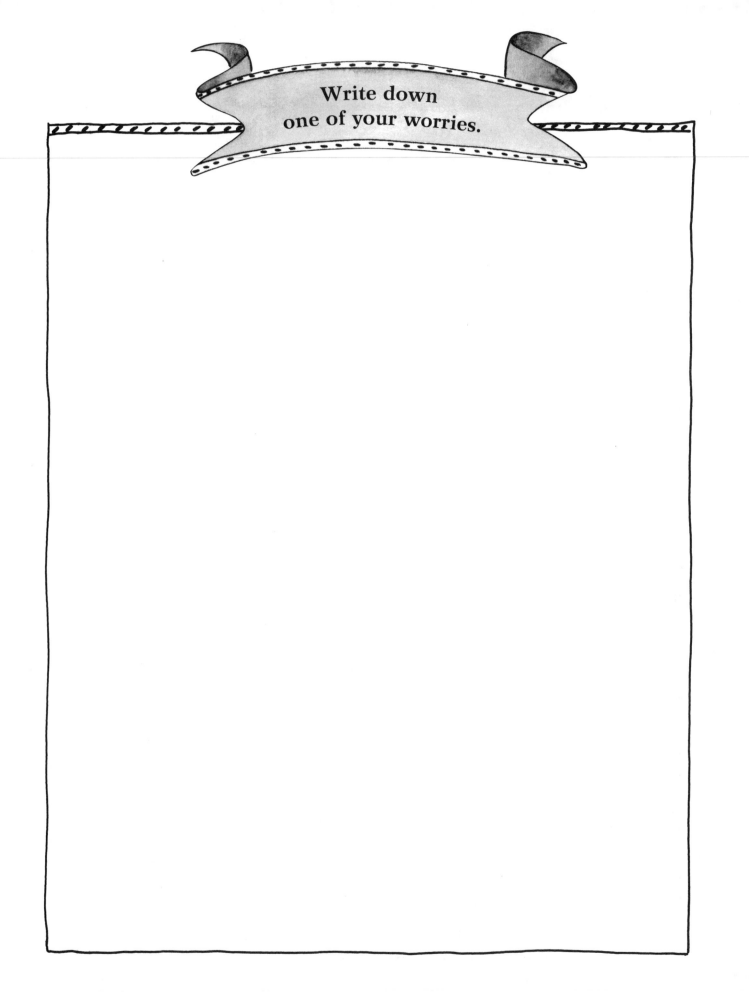

Write down
one of your worries.

**What can you say or do
to help yourself feel
less worried about this?**

Sometimes, even when you have used logic and worked out a plan, or even after your parents have tried to reassure you, the worry just stays in your mind.

When this happens, it's time to think about tomatoes.

CHAPTER FIVE

Spending Less Time on Worries

Remember how worries can be like tomato plants? When you check a tomato plant every day, and water it, and look at the leaves to see if there are little bugs to pick off, you are taking good care of it and helping it grow. When you think about worries a lot and talk about them over and over again, you are helping the worries grow, too.

If you ignore your tomato plant by never giving it water and never checking on it, it will start to wilt, and eventually it will die. The same thing goes for worries. If you don't spend time on them, they will begin to shrivel up and go away.

If you are a person who worries about a lot of little things, try setting up a WORRY TIME. Your mom or dad can help you choose a certain time each day for Worry Time. Worry Time should last about 15 minutes.

Your mom or dad will sit with you during Worry Time and listen to whatever worries you have. There should be no interruptions. No TV. No phone calls. No little brothers wanting to play or big sisters needing help with homework.

Worry Time is the time to say whatever you want to say about your worries. During this special time, your mom or dad will listen and try to help.

Create a sign
for your Worry Time.

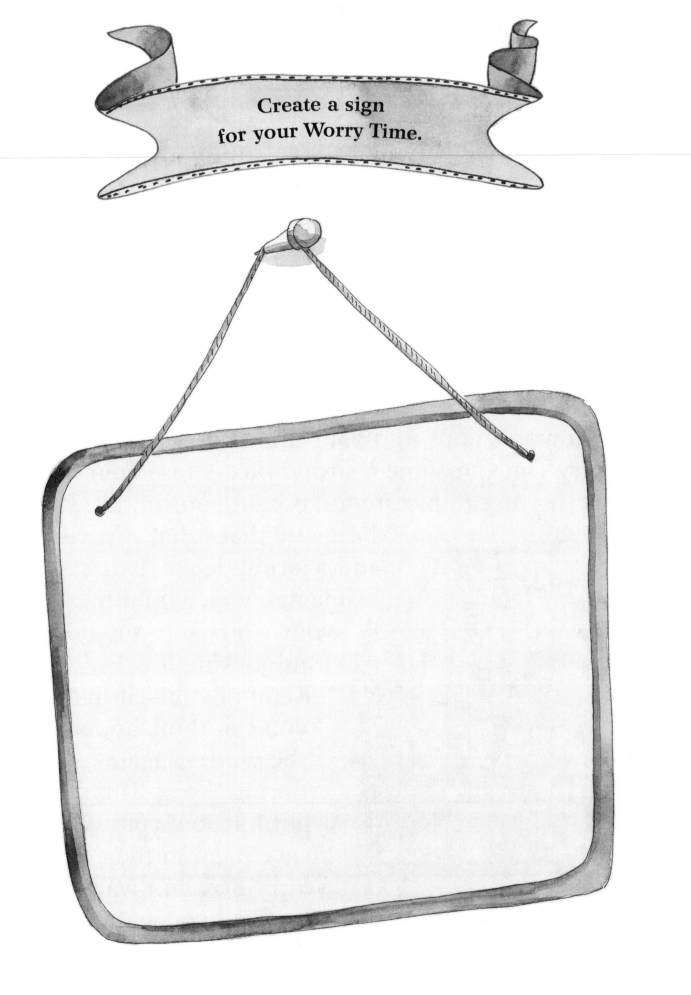

There is just one very important rule about Worry Time:

NO THINKING OR TALKING ABOUT WORRIES UNLESS IT IS WORRY TIME.

If a worry bothers you at any other time of day, you are not allowed to spend time thinking about it or talking about it until Worry Time.

If a worry pops into your mind and it is not Worry Time, imagine a strong box. Close your eyes so you can picture the box in your mind.

Make sure that it has a cover and a strong lock. Then imagine yourself putting your worry into the box and locking it up. Remind yourself that you can think about the worries again during Worry Time, but for now you will leave them in the Worry Box and walk away. Get busy with something else.

Draw the imaginary Worry Box
where you will store your worries.
Remember to make it strong!

If you ask a worry question or tell a worry to your mom or dad and it is not Worry Time, your mom or dad will tell you to put the worry into your Worry Box until it is Worry Time.

Your mom and dad will stop answering your worry questions unless it is Worry Time.

They will stop reassuring you about your worries unless it's Worry Time.

This might seem mean. You are going to be feeling worried and your mom or dad will say, "Oops, that's a worry. Lock it up in your box!" Or they will say, "We can talk about that during Worry Time."

It might feel hard to wait, but really it is for the best, because talking about worries and answering worry questions over and over again whenever they come up is like sprinkling water on a tomato plant all through the day. It will actually make the worries grow like crazy!

When you learn
to put your worries
into the Worry Box
to save them for
Worry Time,
something really
interesting happens.

At first, you
might find that
you can't wait for
Worry Time
because you have
so many worries
to talk about.
It will be hard work
because the worries will
keep coming back into your head and
you'll need to imagine yourself stuffing
them back into the Worry Box a lot.

You will need to keep telling yourself to
wait for Worry Time, over and over again.

But after awhile, you will find that by the time you get to Worry Time, some of the worries will have gone away on their own. You will open up your imaginary Worry Box, and it won't be quite as full as you thought. The silly worries that nag at you—those things you already know but just have to keep asking again and again—those kinds of worries will disappear if you stop paying so much attention to them.

Your Worry Time will change a little. At first you will have tons to talk about, lots of little worries. Then the little worries will go away, and you can use Worry Time to talk about some of the bigger things that might be on your mind.

After awhile, you will find that there aren't big problems to deal with every day, so you can use your Worry Time to just chat with your mom or dad. Your parents should keep spending that 15 minutes with you, but when it isn't filled with worries any more, you might decide to call it something else, like TALK TIME.

CHAPTER SIX

Talking Back to Worries

You have probably noticed that
some worries pop up over and over
again, no matter how many times
you put them into the Worry Box.
It's frustrating, isn't it?

But guess what? There is something
you can do about that. You can learn
to talk back to the worry to make it
go away.

You might already know how to talk
back. Talking back means standing up
for yourself when you don't like what
is going on.

Some kids talk back to their
parents, and that isn't such a good
thing because your parents are there
to help you. But talking back to a
worry is a good thing, because the
worry is just trying to give you a hard
time. The worry is being a BULLY.

Use your imagination to picture
what a worry bully might look like.

Is it a mean, ugly creature with
smelly breath and long claws that
perches on your shoulder and
whispers worry thoughts in your ear?
Or perhaps the worry is a dark blob,
like a cloud person who keeps
raining worries down on you?

Draw what your worry bully looks like.

Do you want that bully hanging around?
No! The only problem is that right now,
the worry bully is stronger than you are.
It knows it, and you know it, too.

But guess what?

You can get stronger.

You can learn to talk
back to the worry.

You can learn to
not give in to it.
You can make it
get off your
shoulder and
go away.

There are a few things you need to remember. The first is this:

WORRIES LIE.

Worry bullies think that it's great fun to trick you, so they exaggerate and lie. Worry bullies want you to believe that the most terrible thing will definitely happen, when really that terrible thing is very unlikely to happen. So keep that in mind. You can't trust a worry bully!

In the past, the worry has made you feel afraid. But now you know about worry bullies. They lie to make you scared.

How do you feel about that worry bully? Are you mad at it? If you are mad, good! Feeling mad can help you feel stronger. It makes it easier to do what you need to do next. You need to talk back.

Turn your head toward your shoulder, where the worry bully is perched, and tell it to GO AWAY. You can say it in your head or say it out loud, but say it like you mean it, in a firm voice.

Tell the worry bully that you don't believe it.

Talking back to the worry is a good thing to do because it makes you more powerful. It makes the worry a little weaker and you a little stronger.

Try it again. Tell the worry to GO AWAY. Tell it:

YOU LIE!
I'M NOT GOING TO LISTEN TO YOU ANY MORE

You can even flick it off your shoulder and imagine it tumbling down to the ground. Squash it with your foot to show it you mean business. Then get busy doing something else. Play with your favorite toy, or watch TV, or ask your parents if you can help make dinner.

The worry bully might continue to talk to you. It wants you to pay attention. Pay attention to something else instead.

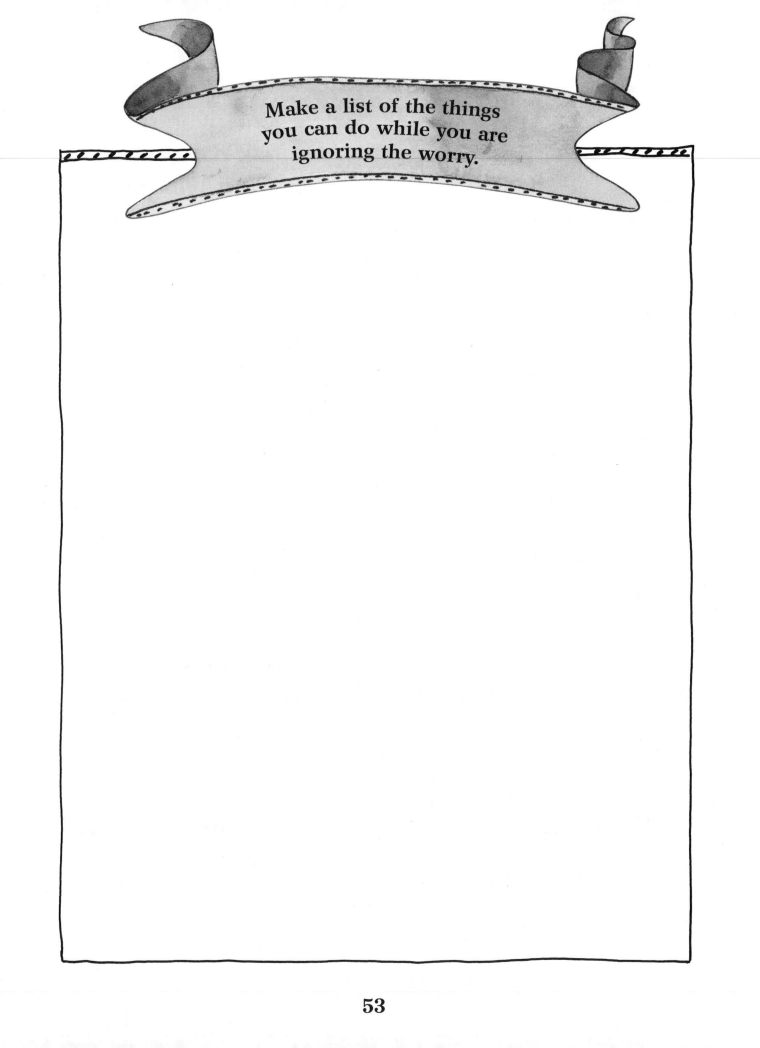

Make a list of the things you can do while you are ignoring the worry.

When you first begin to talk back to the worry, it will probably bother you again pretty quickly. After all, it sees you as a weakling, and it knows you have always listened to it before. So it's probably going to climb right back on your shoulder.

Practice talking back. Say GO AWAY and mean it.

Work hard to get busy with something else so there is less room in your mind for the worry.

Your mom and dad can help, too.

When parents reassure you over and over again about a worry that has gotten stuck in your mind, they're actually helping the worry to be in charge.

Once you start talking back to the worry, your mom and dad should stop answering the same worry questions again and again. Instead, they should remind you that the worry bully is back on your shoulder, whispering worries in your ear.

Your mom and dad can remind you to talk back to the worry. They can help you tell the worry to BUG OFF.

If you do this each time the worry comes, the worry will eventually be too weak to climb back on your shoulder. You can feel proud of yourself when that happens, because it means you've gotten stronger than the worry. You've made the worry go away.

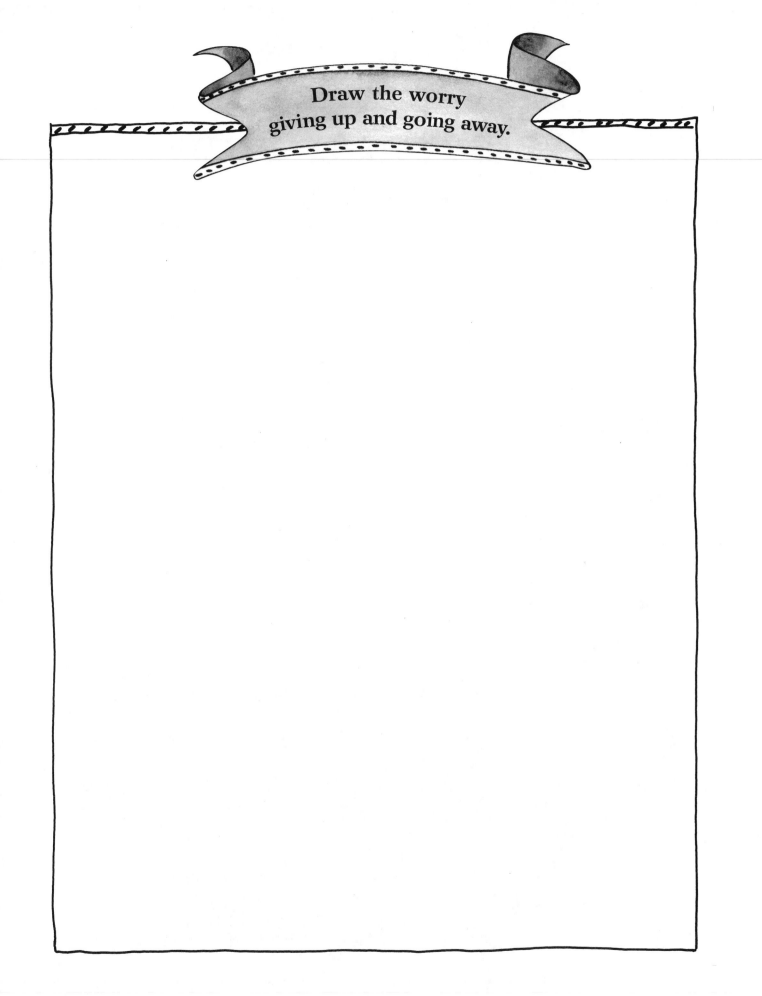

**Draw the worry
giving up and going away.**

Re-setting Your System

Sometimes kids tell the worry to SCRAM, and then they try to play or think about something else, but the worry has already made their whole body feel bad. You can still be in charge, though, because there are plenty of ways to make your body feel okay again.

When a worry has made your body feel bad, you need to do something called "re-setting your system." Re-setting your system means doing something to change the way your body feels.

There are two ways to re-set your system.

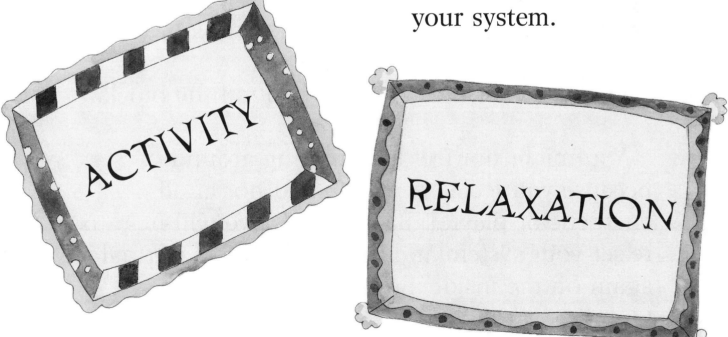

ACTIVITY

When you are worried, things that you cannot see change on the inside of your body. Your heart starts to beat fast, and your stomach might start to hurt. This isn't dangerous, but it feels bad. To get things to go back to normal on the inside, you need to burn off some of the extra energy that is making your body feel strange. The best way to do this is to get involved in something active and fun.

See if you can run up and down the stairs four times before your brother counts to 100.

Roll up a sock and play catch with your dad.

Hop on your bike and ride around the block.

You might not feel like running around because you feel sort of sick and not at all energetic or playful. But being active will help to re-set your system and make things feel normal again on the inside. So talk back to the worry, and then get moving.

Draw or make a list of the active and fun things you can do to re-set your system.

RELAXATION

When worries come in the car or at school, or if it is bedtime or some other time when you can't get active, you can re-set your system in a quieter way. This is called relaxation.

Relaxation means more than just taking a breath. You've probably tried that, and you know it doesn't work. When a worry is jumping around inside you, your brain and your body feel awful. It is hard to just "calm down."

But get ready. You are about to learn a special, quiet way to make your brain and your body feel better.

Let's take it one step at a time,
beginning with your body.

Begin by tensing and relaxing your muscles.

Squeeze your fists.

Make your legs stiff like boards.

Scrunch up your face.

Keep your body tight while you
count to 5 in your head.

Then relax your whole body by
letting your muscles go loose.

Next, think about your breathing. Breathe in through your nose and out through your mouth.

With each breath, picture the air going in through your nose and traveling all the way down toward your belly.

When you are ready,
 breathe out through your mouth.

As you breathe in,
 feel the calm, cool air filling your body.

As you breathe out,
 feel the tense, hot air leaving your body.

In… and out.

In… and out.

In… and out.

In… and out.

In… and out.

Five times altogether.

Now that your body is ready, let's think about your brain. When you're worried, thoughts about the worry take up all of the room in your mind. These worry thoughts keep you feeling bad, even if you have already tried to relax your body.

People might tell you to just not think about the worry, but as you know, that is really hard to do. It's like the worry is being shown on a giant-screen TV in your brain. You can't not watch!

But, you CAN change the channel.

You already know how to change the channel on a real TV. Now you're going to learn how to change the channel in your mind.

Begin by choosing a memory.

Choose one of your most special memories. You probably have a few. Special memories are usually from happy times, when you were having lots of fun or when you succeeded at something that was hard. Maybe you hit a triple in a softball game. Maybe you got to choose your dog from a whole litter of squirming puppies.

Think of a memory that makes you feel really good inside. Remember as many details as you can. What were you wearing? How did the air smell? What could you hear? How did you feel? What did you see?

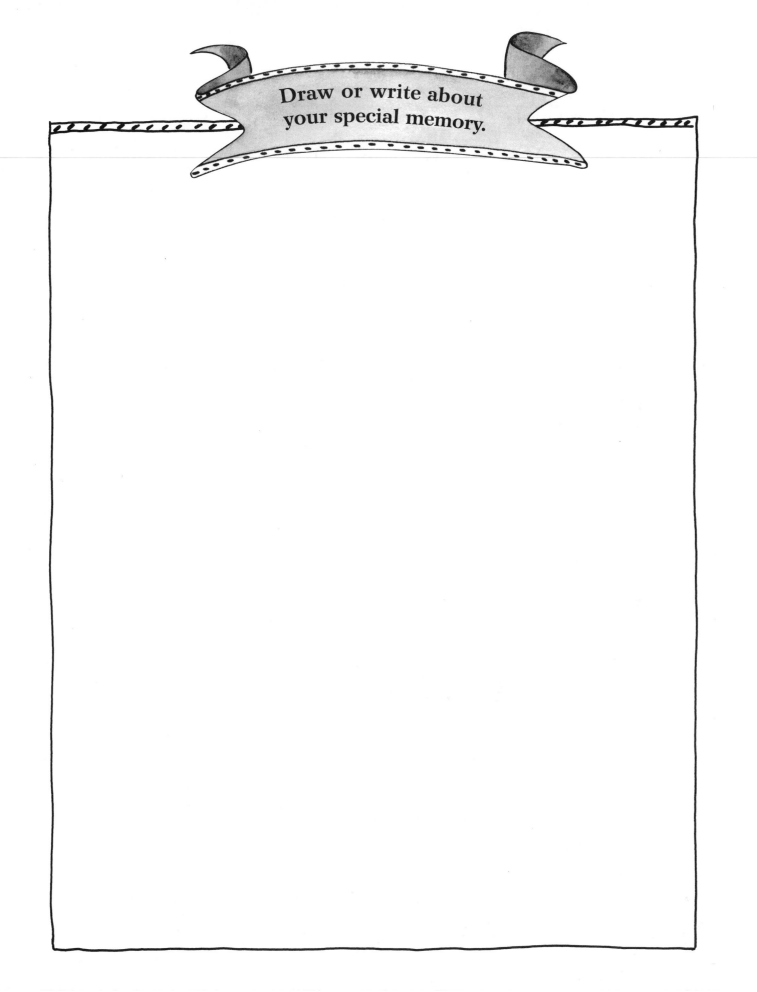

Draw or write about your special memory.

When you practice remembering your special memory, you'll notice that the memory makes you feel better. Just thinking about your favorite memory will help you feel the way you felt that day. It takes practice, but soon you'll notice that you don't just remember feeling happy or excited or proud, you actually feel that way.

And guess what? Feeling happy or excited or proud crowds out the worry! It changes the channel off a worry station and onto one you'd much rather be watching.

Set aside five minutes each day to practice this quiet way of re-setting your system. In the beginning, practice at a time when you aren't busy worrying.

Get your body ready by tightening and relaxing your muscles. Breathe deeply five times (remember to breathe in through your nose and out through your mouth). Then picture your favorite memory in as much detail as you possibly can.

The active way of re-setting your system will work pretty quickly. The quieter way will take some practice, but soon you will find that it works well, too. Take the time to practice so that when a worry comes you'll have a choice about how to help yourself feel better.

CHAPTER EIGHT

Keeping Worries Away

Now that you know a lot about worries and how to get rid of them, there are a few things you should know about keeping worries away.

The first thing to know is that worries have a way of sneaking back up on you.

If you're a person who tends to worry, you'll need to be ready to use your worry-fighting techniques whenever worries begin to bother you.

Taking good care of yourself helps keep you strong for fighting worries. Make sure that you eat healthy foods and get plenty of sleep. It is harder to fight worries when you are hungry or tired.

Keep your body strong by getting exercise every day. Play a sport. Run around at recess. Take the stairs. Use your muscles every day, and your body will have more energy to fight worries.

Think how good you feel after a game of tag or an afternoon of sledding. One of the reasons you feel so good is that exercise helps get rid of stress. Stress is something that can build up when we feel rushed or when we have to work really hard to understand something. Stress can also build up when someone is mad at us or when lots of new things are happening all at once.

When we are stressed, we feel more tired and grouchy. Exercise is a good way to get the stress out so that our bodies and minds can be strong.

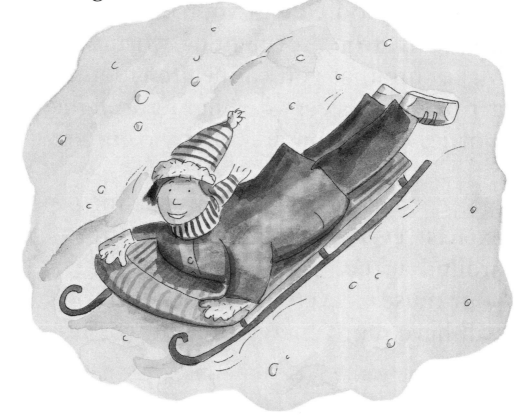

What do you do
to take good care of yourself?

Draw or write
about it here.

Do you remember that worries are like bullies who pick on weak people?

To win the fight against worries, you need to be strong not only in your body but also in your mind. One way to be strong in your mind is to know that you are good at something.

Maybe you are a good friend.

Maybe you get excellent grades in math.

Maybe you score goals when your team plays soccer.

Maybe you are good at drawing horses.

Maybe you sing really nicely.

Find something that you are good at, and then do that thing. Be proud of yourself for what you are good at. And talk about your strengths with the grown-ups in your life.

Knowing that there are some things you are good at helps you feel more confident that you can learn to be good at fighting worries.

Draw yourself doing something you are good at.

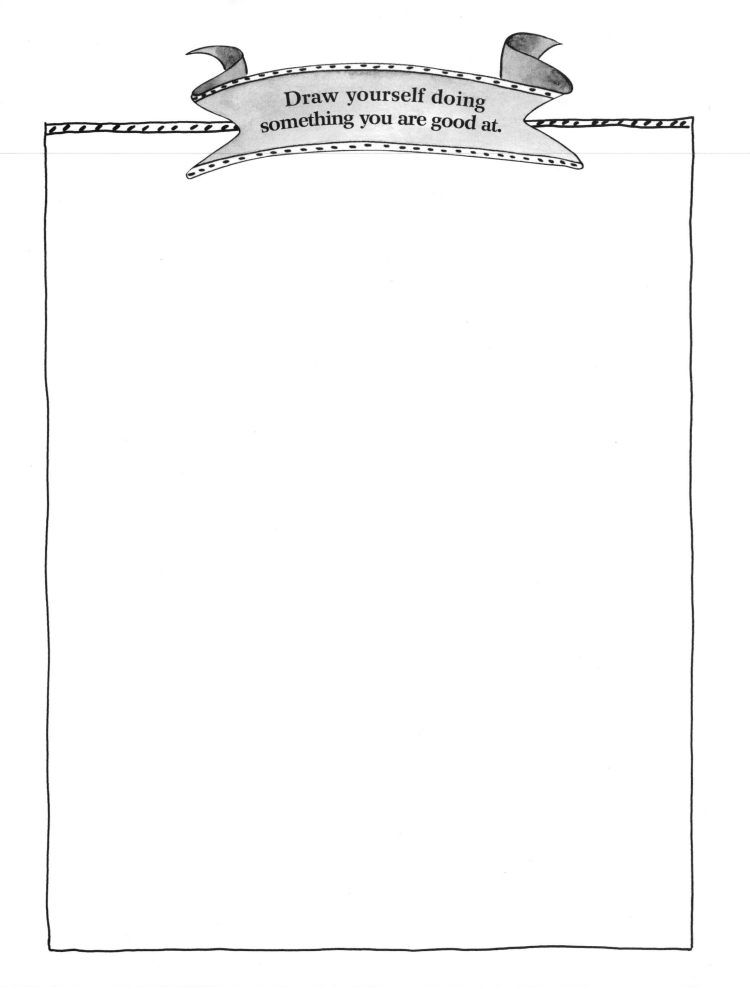

You Can Do It!

Fighting worries is hard work at the start.

The worries are used to having you listen to them. But you can change that.

The more you practice the ideas described in this book, the stronger you will become. And the stronger you are, the weaker the worries will be.

Now you are stronger because you know what to do.

HOW TO BEAT THE WORRIES

Use logic against worries.

Lock worries up in a strong box in your mind.

Make worries wait for Worry Time.

Tell worries to GET LOST!

Move your body to re-set your system.

Relax with a favorite memory.

Stay strong in your body and your mind.

Now that you are stronger, fighting worries will be easier. You can be a kid who isn't bothered most of the time by worries.

Imagine yourself as that kind of kid.

Imagine yourself being strong enough to tell your worries to go away.

Imagine the worries actually going away.

**Draw yourself
without your worries.**

It is going to feel so good!